REGULAR SHOW™

A CARTOON NETWORK ORIGINAL

PARKS AND WRECK

REGULAR

A CARTOON NETWORK

CREATED BY JG QUINTEL

"SKY KICKS"

SCRIPT BY **KEVIN BURKHALTER**
ART BY **TESSA STONE**
LETTERS BY **COREY BREEN**

"WI-FI MADNESS"

SCRIPT BY **YUMI SAKUGAWA**
ART BY **ALLISON STREJLAU**
COLORS BY **LISA MOORE**

"VIDEO GAME GENIE"

SCRIPT BY **JIMMY GIEGERICH**
ART BY **MAD RUPERT**
COLORS BY **WHITNEY COGAR**

"MUSCLE SCOUTS"

BY **ANDY KLUTHE**

"SPRING EQUI-NOT"

BY **MOLLY OSTERTAG**

"FLIGHT FIGHT"

SCRIPT BY **KEVIN PANETTA**
ART BY **RIAN SYGH**
COLORS AND LETTERS BY **KATY FARINA**

"COUSIN GEOFF"

BY **KRISTINA NESS**
LETTERS BY **SHAWN ALDRIDGE**

"MELAN COLLIE"

SCRIPT BY **SHANNA MATUSZAK**
ART BY **DEREK CHARM**
LETTERS BY **JIM CAMPBELL**

"RE-BIRTHDAY"

SCRIPT BY **DEREK FRIDOLFS**
AND **PAMELA LOVAS**
ART BY **TERRY BLAS**
LETTERS BY **ED DUKESHIRE**

"GHOST GENESIS MECHA FIGHT"

SCRIPT AND ART BY **SARA GOETTER**
COLORS BY **JEN HICKMAN**
LETTERS BY **ED DUKESHIRE**

ROSS RICHIE CEO & Founder • MATT GAGNON Editor-in-Chief • FILIP SABLIK President of Publishing & Marketing • STEPHEN CHRISTY President of Development • LANCE KREITER VP of Licensing & Merchandising
PHIL BARBARO VP of Finance • ARUNE SINGH VP of Marketing • BRYCE CARLSON Managing Editor • MEL CAYLO Marketing Manager • SCOTT NEWMAN Production Design Manager
KATE HENNING Operations Manager • SIERRA HAHN Senior Editor • DAFNA PLEBAN Editor, Talent Development • SHANNON WATTERS Editor • ERIC HARBURN Editor • WHITNEY LEOPARD Editor • JASMINE AMIRI Editor
CHRIS ROSA Associate Editor • ALEX GALER Associate Editor • CAMERON CHITTOCK Associate Editor • MATTHEW LEVINE Assistant Editor • SOPHIE PHILIPS-ROBERTS Assistant Editor
JILLIAN CRAB Production Designer • MICHELLE ANKLEY Production Designer • KARA LEOPARD Production Designer • GRACE PARK Production Design Assistant • ELIZABETH LOUGHRIDGE Accounting Coordinator
STEPHANIE HOCUTT Social Media Coordinator • JOSÉ MEZA Event Coordinator • HOLLY AITCHISON Operations Assistant • MEGAN CHRISTOPHER Operations Assistant • MORGAN PERRY Direct Market Representative

REGULAR SHOW: Parks and Wreck, November 2017. Published by KaBOOM!, a division of Boom Entertainment, Inc. REGULAR SHOW, CARTOON
NETWORK, the logos, and all related characters and elements are trademarks of and © Cartoon Network. (S17) Originally published in single
magazine form as REGULAR SHOW 2014 ANNUAL No. 1, REGULAR SHOW 2015 SPECIAL No. 1, REGULAR SHOW 2017 SPECIAL No. 1. © Cartoon
Network. (S17) All rights reserved. KaBOOM!™ and the KaBOOM! logo are trademarks of Boom Entertainment, Inc., registered in various
countries and categories. All characters, events, and institutions depicted herein are fictional. Any similarity between any of the names,
characters, persons, events, and/or institutions in this publication to actual names, characters, and persons, whether living or dead, events,
and/or institutions is unintended and purely coincidental. KaBOOM! does not read or accept unsolicited submissions of ideas, stories, or artwork.

BOOM! Studios, 5670 Wilshire Boulevard, Suite 450, Los Angeles, CA 90036-5679. Printed in China. First Printing.

ISBN: 978-1-68415-042-7, eISBN: 978-1-61398-719-3

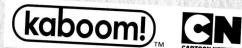

SHOW™

ORIGINAL

COVER BY

JORGE CORONA
WITH COLORS BY **JEN HICKMAN**

DESIGNER
GRACE PARK

ASSISTANT EDITORS
SOPHIE PHILIPS-ROBERTS
& MARY GUMPORT

EDITORS
SIERRA HAHN
SHANNON WATTERS &
WHITNEY LEOPARD

WITH SPECIAL THANKS TO
MARISA MARIONAKIS, JANET NO, CURTIS LELASH, CONRAD MONTGOMERY, KELLY
CREWS, RYAN SLATER AND THE WONDERFUL FOLKS AT CARTOON NETWORK.

SKY KICKS

WRITTEN BY KEVIN BURKHALTER
ILLUSTRATED BY TESSA STONE

WI-FI MADNESS
WRITTEN BY YUMI SAKUGAWA
ILLUSTRATED BY ALLISON STREJLAU

DUDE, WE ARE SOOOOO CLOSE TO OVERTHROWING THE ZOMBIE DEMON OVERLORD.

WHAT ARE YOU DOING, MAN? CAST THE FIREBALL SPELL. *THE FIREBALL SPE--*

NOOOOOOOOOOO!!!

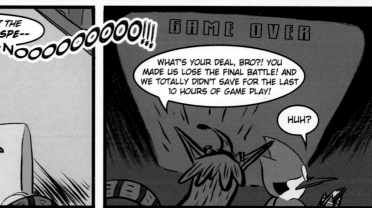

GAME OVER

WHAT'S YOUR DEAL, BRO?! YOU MADE US LOSE THE FINAL BATTLE! AND WE TOTALLY DIDN'T SAVE FOR THE LAST 10 HOURS OF GAME PLAY!

HUH?

EVER SINCE WE WON THOSE COOL SMART PHONES IN THAT FLAMING HOT CHIPS BARCODE GIVEAWAY, YOU'VE BEEN DOING NOTHING BUT PLAY WITH YOUR SMART PHONE ALL DAY.

WHATEVER, RIGBY, YOU'RE THE ONE TO TALK. YOU HAVE YOUR SMART PHONE TAPED ONTO YOUR TAIL 24/7 WAITING FOR SOMEBODY TO SEND YOU A DIGIPAL REQUEST. AND LAST TIME I CHECKED, YOUR NUMBER OF DIGIPAL REQUESTS HAVE BEEN *ZERO*.

DIGIPAL REQUESTS: 0

SHUT UP, DUDE! THAT IS LIKE TOTALLY NONE OF YOUR BUSINESS!

OKAY, EASY BRO...

YOU'RE THE WEIRDO WHO'S OBSESSED WITH HIS SMART PHONE, NOT ME! I BET I CAN TOTALLY GO FOR LONGER WITHOUT A SMART PHONE THAN YOU!

DID YOU SAY...BET?

OKAY, HERE ARE THE RULES OF THE BET. NO SMART PHONE, INTERNET--

--OR VIDEO GAMES.

FIRST PERSON TO TOUCH ANY ELECTRONIC DEVICE...

TOTALLY OWES THE OTHER PERSON A CHEESE-STUFFED PASTRY CRUST PEPPERONI BURGER PIZZA FROM PETE'S PIZZA.

READY OR NOT, ANALOG LIFE, HERE I COME.

I'M GOING TO TOTALLY BUST ALL MY FINGERS FROM CAR-PAYING ALL THAT DIEM.

10 MINUTES LATER...

UH...I WOULD HATE TO BE ONE OF THOSE LAME-OS WHO IS SO ADDICTED TO THE INTERNET...

...THAT HE STARTS HALLUCINATING ALL KINDS OF WEIRD THINGS...

...LIKE IMAGINING THAT THAT TREE OVER THERE HAS TURNED INTO A WI-FI SIGNAL AND IS NOW MORPHING INTO AN EVIL MONSTER COMING TOWARDS US...

WAIT, YOU SEE IT TOO?!

UH...I DON'T KNOW WHAT YOU'RE TALKING ABOUT!

DID SOMEBODY SUMMON ME?

UH. I DON'T THINK SO?

I'M HERE TO HELP YOU WITH YOUR BAD CASE OF *FOMO!*

FOMO: Fear Of Missing Out

TO PLUG YOU BACK INTO THE ONLINE WORLD WHERE YOU BELONG!

HEY MAN, THIS IS TOTALLY SOMETHING BETWEEN ME AND MY BUD. WE REALLY DON'T NEED YOUR INVOLVEMENT.

FOOL! I AM YOUR FRIEND, YOU SEE? I WANT TO *SAVE* YOU FROM THE SHEER BOREDOM OF LIVING COMPLETELY IN THE OFFLINE WORLD. SO *BORING*, ISN'T IT?

UMM, YEAH, A LITTLE BIT.

ALL THE MOVIE TRAILERS YOU WANT IN STREAMING HD!

EVERY VERSION OF EVERY VIDEO GAME EVER INVENTED!

LIVE STREAMS OF ROCK BAND CONCERTS BEFORE THEY EVEN PERFORM!

ALL YOU NEED TO DO IS TO CLIMB THE CRYSTAL PIXEL STAIRCASE TO THE ETERNAL DIGITAL AFTERLIFE...

AND STAY CONNECTED FOREVER WHERE YOU WILL NEVER EXPERIENCE BOREDOM OR LONELINESS OR WORK

EVER AGAIN.

SUCH MORTAL IDIOTS! LITTLE DO THEY KNOW THAT ONCE THEY ENTER THE DIGITAL AFTERLIFE I WILL SUCK THEIR ANALOG SOULS DRY AND ENSLAVE THEM AS INTERNET TROLLS FOR THE REST OF THEIR LIVES!

BWA HA HA HA HA HA!

MAN, THE WI-FI DEVIL MUST THINK WE'RE SOOOO DUMB IF HE'S GOING TO TELL US HOW HE'S GOING TO STEAL OUR SOULS RIGHT WITHIN OUR EARSHOT.

VIDEO GAMES! GETTING TO GLOAT ABOUT YOUR MAD SKILLS TO RANDOM JEALOUS STRANGERS! WOO-WOO!

DOES THIS MEAN WE ARE NEVER GOING TO SEE OUR RL FRIENDS AGAIN?

WE CAN SEND THEM E-MAILS OR PLAY VIDEO GAMES WITH THEM, DUH!

OH. RIGHT!

YOU HAVE EVERYTHING YOU NEED! EVERYTHING YOUR HEART DESIRES FOREVER AND EVER!

SO LONG, BORING REAL LIFE.

THANKS FOR NOTH— WAIT, DO YOU SMELL THAT?

IT'S PIZZA. I SMELL PIZZA.

WE WERE SUPPOSED TO EAT PIZZA AFTER THIS STUPID BET!

YOU KNOW WHAT, RIGBY? IT IS SO IMPORTANT TO COMPLETELY UNPLUG FROM TIME TO TIME... BECAUSE OTHERWISE YOU TURN INTO AN INTERNET-OBSESSED TOOL AND EVERYONE HATES YOU.

YEAH, I MEAN TECHNICALLY YOU CAN EAT PIZZA AND PLAY VIDEO GAMES AT THE SAME TIME...

BUT THEN THAT MEANS YOU SORT OF SUCK AT BOTH ACTIVITIES AT ONCE.

DO YOU KNOW WHAT I THINK WE NEED TO DO?

WHAT?

TIME TO TURN THESE *SMART* PHONES...INTO *DUMB* PHONES.

DUDE, WHAT ARE YOU DOING?!

WE'RE GOING TO LIVE COMPLETELY OFF THE GRID, JUST LIKE OUR ANCESTORS DID! UNPLUGGED LIFE, HERE WE COME!

YOU IDIOT! HOW ARE WE SUPPOSED TO FIND OUR WAY HOME NOW?

UH...

THE END.

VIDEO GAME GENIE

WRITTEN BY JIMMY GIEGERICH

ILLUSTRATED BY MAD RUPERT

PFWOO~

WHO HATH SUMMONED THE GENIE OF THE UN-MARKED CARTRIDGE??

UH... MORDECAI...

R-RIGBY...

GREETINGS, MORDECAI AND RIGBY!

I THANK YOU FOR FREEING ME FROM MY 8-BIT PRISON!

SO...WANNA SEE WHAT OTHER GAMES ARE IN THE BOX?

SURE!

WIP

I KNOW SOME AWESOME CHEATS FOR STREET PUNCHER!

PUNCH!

EH...BEEN THERE, DONE THAT.

LET'S PLAY IT THE WAY IT WAS MEANT TO BE PLAYED.

YEAH!

WITH CHEAT CODES!

DUH!

THE END!

OH, *JEFF*, PICNIC NACHOS ARE THE BEST KIND OF NACHOS.

NO, SUZY, THE BEST KIND OF NACHOS...

...ARE NACHOS SHARED WITH YOU.

OH NO, BRO!

A BEAR!

W-WHERE IS IT, JEFF?!

I... I DON'T KNOW!

IN THE WILD THERE IS ONLY ONE RULE:

FINDERS, KEEPERS.

THIS IS PART OF A LESSON I CALL *FORAGING FOR NACHOS*.

IF YOU FOLLOW IT, NATURE WILL *ALWAYS* KEEP YOU *WELL FED* AND *SMOTHERED WITH CHEESE*.

THE END

FLIGHT FIGHT

Written by Kevin Panetta   Drawn by Rian Sygh
Colors and Letters by Katy Farina

MY ITEMIZED HULA HOOP INVOICE!

SWINGING HIPS HULA EMPORIUM

ITEM	DESCRIPTION	
RED	A RED HOOP!	
BLUE	A BLUE HOOP!	
FLAME	FLAMIN' COOL!	1

What kind of MONSTER would create a TOY out of my BEAUTIFUL PAPERWORK?

Hey! Who threw that?!

What in the blue blazes?

Okay! We are about to start round two of the Park's First Annual Paper Airplane Tournament!

PAPER PLANE CONTEST

But before we get back to the action, I'd like to say a few words about the journey that brought us here. See, ever since me and Mordecai were a couple of wide-eyed youths, we have DREAMED about the miracle of flight!

Today...

sniff

...We make that dream reality.

The rules are simple. It's an eight-man single-elimination tournament. Whoever can throw a paper airplane the farthest wins.

Round two is about to begin, dudes. The competition has been rough so far, especially for some of you.

I'm looking at you, God of Basketball.

Paper planes are NOT my game. I'm willing to admit that.

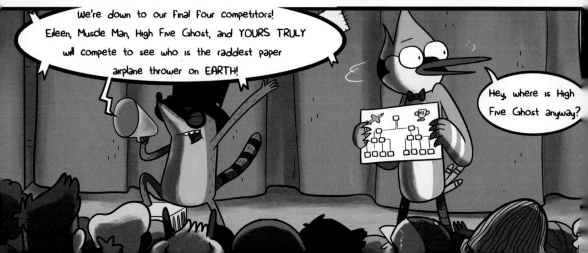

We're down to our final four competitors! Eileen, Muscle Man, High Five Ghost, and YOURS TRULY will compete to see who is the raddest paper airplane thrower on EARTH!

Hey, where is High Five Ghost anyway?

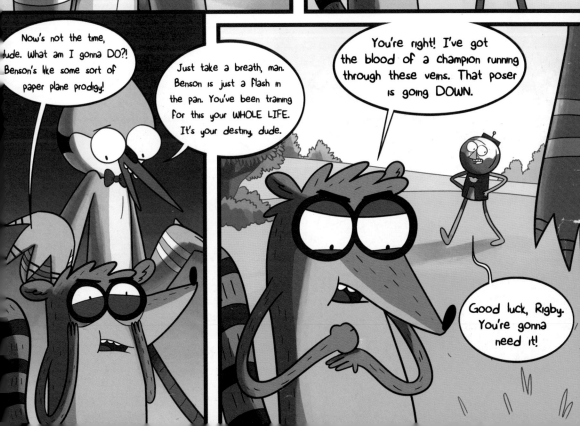

THE END

COUSIN GEOFF

WRITTEN AND ILLUSTRATED
BY KRISTINA NESS
LETTERS BY
SHAWN ALDRIDGE

AHHHHH!

'SUP, NERDS?

OH, HEY! GEOFF!

RIGBY, THIS IS MY COUSIN GEOFF! HE'S CANADIAN.

ACTUALLY, WHY AREN'T YOU IN CANADA?

WELL, MY SIDE OF THE FAMILY MIGRATES SOUTH EVERY WINTER.

AND SEEING AS I'M ON MY WAY NORTH FOR THE SUMMER ANYWAY, I FIGURED I'D STOP BY AND GIVE MY SECOND-FAVORITE LITTLE COUSIN A VISIT.

SECOND-FAVORITE...?

SO, YEAH. THIS IS OUR PLACE. YOU CAN CRASH HERE ON THE COUCH FOR THE NIGHT.

YEAH, THIS'LL DO FOR A WHILE.

UH, HOW LONG ARE YOU STAYING ANYWAY?

JUST A FEW DAYS TO REST MY ARMS. FIRST CLASS CAN REALLY BE A PAIN, KNOW WHAT I MEAN?

BUT YOU WOULDN'T KNOW WHAT THAT'S LIKE, WOULD YOU, BRO?

RIGBY AND I HAVE WORK IN THE MORNING, SO WE'RE GOING TO HIT THE SACK.

I'LL STAY UP A BIT AND PLAY SOME GAMES.

8 HOURS LATER.

ZAP PEW PEW PEW

UGH, HOW LATE WAS GEOFF UP LAST NIGHT? I BARELY SLEPT.

I SLEPT JUST FINE, DUDE.

MY BREAD! DID YOU EAT THE REST OF MY TOAST BREAD!?

NO WAY!

DUDE, CHECK OUT YOUR *BUTT!*

GEOFF...

MY BUTT!

AH, PARDON ME, GOOD MORNING. DO YOU REALIZE THAT THERE ARE...*DROPPINGS* ON OUR FRONT PORCH?

GEOFF--!

WHOA NOW, DUDE. LET'S JUST GO TO WORK AND DEAL WITH THE GEOFF PROBLEM LATER.

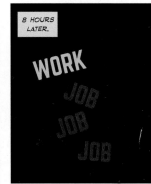

8 HOURS LATER.

WORK JOB JOB JOB

MY VIDEOGAMES!

OH, HEY GUYS.

BUT MY--!

DRAG

DRAG

DUDE, WE *HAVE* TO GET RID OF GEOFF.

HE'S GOTTA GO.

OHHHHHHH!

DUDE, NOTHING'S WORKING!

IT'S LIKE GEOFF IS SO ANNOYING THAT HE DEFLECTS WHATEVER ANNOYING THINGS WE DO TO HIM!

AT THIS RATE, HE'LL BE HERE 'TIL NEXT WINTER!

BUURP

'TIL NEXT WINTER, HMMM?

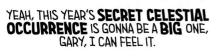

YEAH, THIS YEAR'S **SECRET CELESTIAL OCCURRENCE** IS GONNA BE A **BIG** ONE, GARY, I CAN FEEL IT.

OH, DON'T WORRY! I HAVE SOMETHING REALLY SPECIAL FOR THIS ASTROLOGICAL, ERR, UH, "HAPPENING"!

WE'LL BE ABLE TO SEE **TOMORROW** WITH THE NEW EQUIPMENT I GOT.

JUST MAKE SURE YOU, **DEATH,** AND THE **GUARDIANS OF ETERNAL YOUTH** ARE ON TIME. CARPOOL IF YOU GOTTA.

OH, UHH, 11PM SHARP!

SAME SPOT AS LAST YEAR.

HERE YOU GO, PUT THESE ON AND BRACE YOURSELVES.

YOU THINK EILEEN IS MAD?

WOULDN'T **YOU** BE, DUDE? WE DITCHED HER TO GO EAT **HOT DOGS.** WE SHOULDA' KEPT OUR PLANS.

BUT UNLIMITED HOT DOGS!

POP!

OW!

UMM, EILEEN?

MORDECAI, WHY IS IT SO DARK IN HERE?

I DON'T KNOW MAN, FIND A LAMP OR SOMETHING.

EILEEN? ARE YOU HERE? WE CAME TO SAY **SORRY.**

DON'T TOUCH THAT!

EI-EILEEN! HEEEYY, DIDN'T SEE YOU IN HERE, *HEH HEH...*

OH, YOU DIDN'T SEE ME? LIKE, I'M **INVISIBLE?**

N-NO! I JUST MEANT I WAS SURPRISED! EILEEN, WE'RE REALLY SORRY. WE SHOULDN'T HAVE FORGOTTEN--

IT'S TOO LATE FOR "SORRY"! WHAT HAS MANIFESTED CANNOT BE UNDONE--I AM AN **ENIGMA,** A BARREN DESERT LACKING THE ABILITY TO FEEL ANYTHING OTHER THAN COMPLETE **DISCONNECTION** AND AN INTENSE URGE TO PAINT MY FINGERNAILS BLACK. YOU CAN'T POSSIBLY UNDERSTAND--

NOW, RIGBY! THROW THE STICK!

CHUCK!

UGGGHHHH, WHAT HAPPENED?

EW! BLACK FINGERNAIL POLISH!?

SKIPS, WHERE DID YOU GET THE AWESOME MAGICAL DISTRACTION ROD?

OH, THAT WAS JUST A REGULAR STICK. DOGS LIKE STICKS.

END.

REBIRTHDAY

STORY BY DEREK FRIDOLFS AND PAMELA LOVAS

SCRIPT BY DEREK FRIDOLFS

ART BY TERRY BLAS

LETTERS BY ED DUKESHIRE

NO WAY. WHY WOULD HE LIE TO ME?

HE DIDN'T JUST LIE TO YOU, MORDECAI. HE LIED TO ALL OF US.

I JUST HOPE IT'S NOT TOO LATE FOR ME TO RETURN THAT CAKE.

HISSSSSSS

RIGBY, STOP!

BACK OFF, MAN! I'LL DO IT! YOU KNOW I'LL DO IT!

RIGBY! **NO!** I'M WARNING YOU...DON'T--

BLOOOOOW

AAAAAA

HELLO?

HAPPY BIRTHDAY, RIGBY!!

GUYS, IT WORKED! YOU'RE ALL HERE!

OF COURSE, RIGBY. WE WOULDN'T FORGET YOUR BIRTHDAY.

I MEAN, YOU'RE ALL BACK. I TOTALLY WISHED YOU ALL AWAY.

YOU DID WHAT NOW?

I DIDN'T MEAN TO. BUT I LIED ABOUT MY BIRTHDAY. AND ALL OF YOU KEPT GIVING ME CAKE AND PRESENTS. I COULDN'T HELP MYSELF! AND THEN I MADE YOU DISAPPEAR. BUT NOW YOU'RE BACK. AND I PROMISE I'LL NEVER DO IT AGAIN.

OK...STOP BEING WEIRD AND JUST FEAST YOUR EYES OVER THERE.

...OH NO...

GHOST GENESIS MECHA FIGHT

SCRIPT AND ART BY SARA GOETTER
COLORS BY JEN HICKMAN
LETTERS BY ED DUKESHIRE

HIGH FIVE GHOST.

IT'S TIME.

PIF

YOU MUSTN'T RUN AWAY, BRO!

NOOOOO!

I'M SCARED! WAHHHH!!

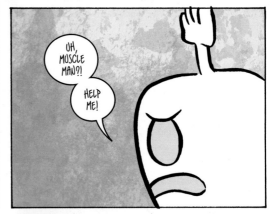

THE CASE OF
HIGH FIVE GHOST

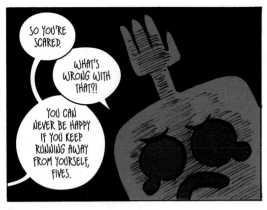

THE END

ROLLER RIGBY

SCRIPT AND ART BY KRISTIN KEMPER
LETTERS BY ED DUKESHIRE

HEY, MORDECAI, CHECK THIS OUT!

SUMMER SKATE-OFF

at the

MIDTOWN ROLLER RINK

COOL PRIZES!!!

*o

FOR

COULD BE YOUR CHANCE FOR YOUR BIG COMEBACK, HUH? HUH?

DUDE, NOT SO LOUD! I NEVER SHOULD HAVE TOLD YOU ABOUT MY TRAGIC BACKSTORY.

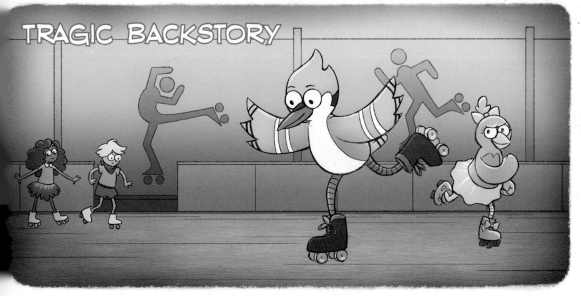

TRAGIC BACKSTORY

THE NEXT DAY

TIME FOR A TRAINING MONTAGE!

THE END

FANCY DINNER

SCRIPT AND ART BY
HANNAH BLUMENREICH

COLORS BY
FRED C. STRESING

LETTERS BY
ED DUKESHIRE

I'M TOTALLY STUFFED, THAT WAS AMAZING!

WELL, IT OUGHT TO BE, I SPENT WEEKS TRACKING DOWN SOME OF THESE RECIPES.

WEEKS?

SURE. THE SHEPHERD'S PIE WAS AN OLD RECIPE OF MY GRANDMOTHER'S. I FOUND IT WEDGED IN ONE OF HER OLD SCRAPBOOKS ABOUT DONALD PLEASENCE.

DON'T KNOW WHY.

ANYWAY, PLANNING THIS NICE DINNER MEANT A LOT TO ME.

RRRGGGGHHHH

I'VE BEEN TRYING ALL DAY AND I JUST CAN'T GET IT!!

WHOA, DUDE, CALM DOWN! WHAT'S GOING ON?

YOU'RE JUST GONNA LAUGH AT ME.

I CAN'T LAUGH IF I DON'T KNOW WHAT'S GOING ON.

[EI]LEEN MADE ME THIS REAL [N]ICE DINNER LAST NIGHT [A]ND I FELT BAD BECAUSE [I] NEVER DO NICE THINGS [F]OR HER SO I WANTED TO MAKE A NICE DINNER BACK.

SHE EVEN MADE SOME FANCY DONALD PLEASENCE SHEPHERD'S PIE! IT WAS HER GRANDMOTHER'S RECIPE!

WHO'S DONALD PLEASENCE?

DING-DONG

WHAT, UH... HAPPENED?

I WANTED TO MAKE A NICE DINNER LIKE THE ONE YOU MADE FOR ME! I HAD IT ALL PLANNED OUT, BUT NONE OF IT WENT RIGHT.

I'M... A TERRIBLE BOYFRIEND.

AW, RIGBY, YOU'RE NOT A TERRIBLE BOYFRIEND!

REALLY?

HAVE YOU EVER COOKED BEFORE?

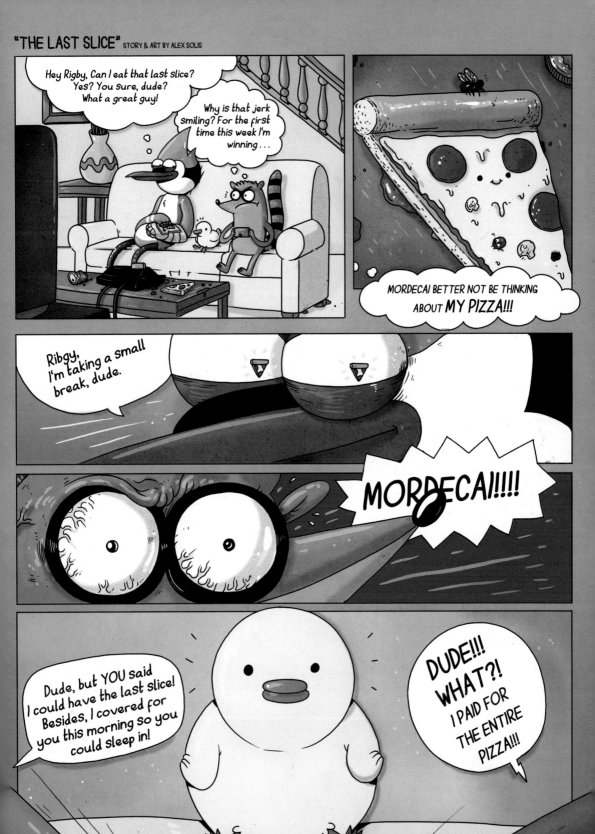

END!

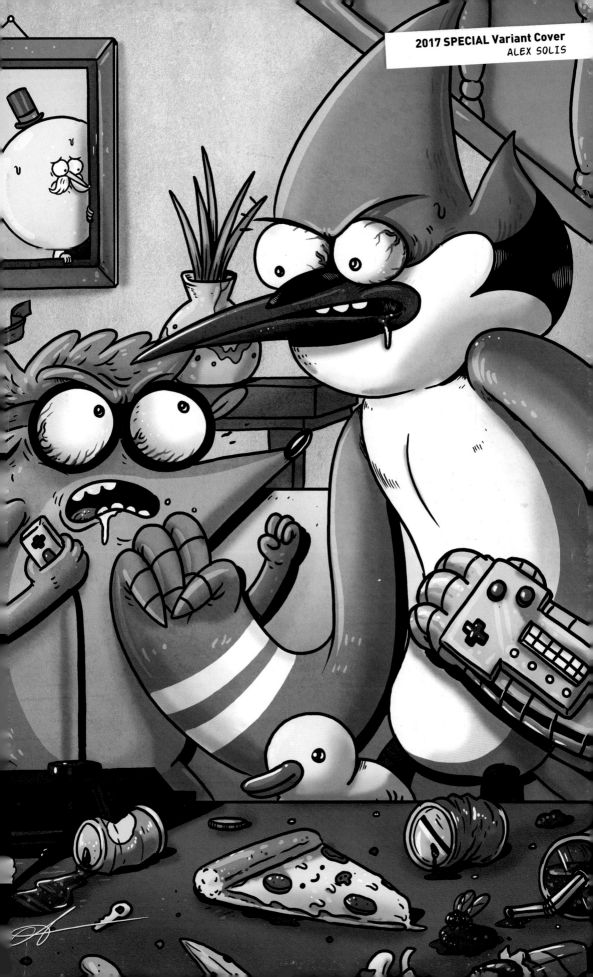

2017 SPECIAL Variant Cover
ALEX SOLIS

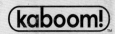